Meep
and the
Midnight Mess

Written by Tarnelia Matthews
Illustrated by Danielle Arrington

Collins

Nora is off to bed.

3

Kit pads in. He is looking for food.

Meep looks on in shock!

Meep runs up to the bedroom.

Nora sighs.

Nora sees the mess.

She sees Kit too!

"Shoo, Kit! Shoo!" yells Nora.

Midnight mess

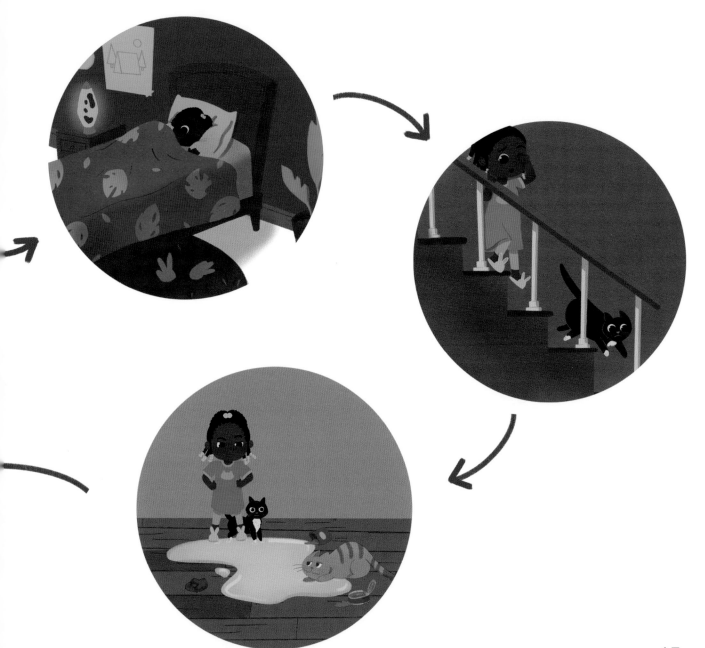

Review: After reading

Use your assessment from hearing the children read to choose any GPCs, words or tricky words that need additional practice.

Read 1: Decoding

- Ask the children to read Nora's speech bubble on page 9. Ask: What does **all right** mean? (*okay*)
  - Ask: What else can the word "right" mean? Prompt with example phrases: *my right hand*; *my answer was right*.
- Ask the children to read the following words. Check they sound out the long /oo/ and short /**oo**/ sounds correctly.

  bedroom   **looking**   **shoo**   **good**   **food**   **too**

- Turn to page 6 and challenge the children to sound out the words silently in their heads first, so that they can read the sentence aloud fluently.

Read 2: Prosody

- Model reading page 12, and talk about the meaning of the word **shoo**. (e.g. *go away, get out*)
- Ask the children to experiment saying "shoo" in a dramatic way, imagining that they are shooing a cat out of the classroom.

Read 3: Comprehension

- Hold a class discussion about cats. Encourage the children to talk about a cat's needs, such as food, water and a cat flap to go in and out of their home.
- Read the back cover blurb. Can the children answer the question: **Was it Meep?** Encourage them to explain their answer.
- Focus on the character of Meep.
  - On page 5, ask: How is Meep feeling? (*shocked*) Why? (e.g. *because Kit is tipping food off the counter*)
  - On page 6, ask: Why is Meep mee-owing? (e.g. *to wake Nora up*)
  - On page 9, ask: What do you think Meep wants Nora to do? (e.g. *go downstairs and stop Kit*)
  - On page 13, ask: What does Nora think of Meep? Why? (*that Meep is a good cat, because Meep told Nora that Kit was making a mess*)
- Turn to pages 14–15 and ask the children to recall the story in their own words using the pictures as prompts.